THE MIND IN WORDS AND ACTIONS

Preliminary Remarks Concerning Two Diagrams

THE MIND IN WORDS AND ACTIONS

Preliminary Remarks Concerning Two Diagrams

Arthur Schnitzler

TRANSLATED, WITH AN
INTRODUCTION, BY *Robert O. Weiss*

Frederick Ungar Publishing Co., New York

Translated from Arthur Schnitzler's
Der Geist im Wort und der Geist in der Tat
and published by arrangement
with S. Fischer Associates, Inc.

Contents

Introduction

IN HIS LITERARY CAREER of more than forty
years, Arthur Schnitzler (1862–1931) had to
contend with many vehement attacks on his work
by malicious critics. They employed every means
at their command to discredit him—including
deliberate omissions of essential elements in
their descriptions of his works, outright mis-
quotations, and false or misleading statements
about him. Why was he subjected to so much
unfair criticism?

In Schnitzler's Austria, a writer whose social
and psychological insights were decades ahead
of his time, one, moreover, who was not to be
deterred from his ceaseless pursuit of the truth
and from communicating his findings to the
theatergoing and reading public, was sure to
incur the hostility of the powerful adherents of
a hyperconservative establishment. If he was,
like Schnitzler, a Jew as well, anti-Semitic voices
would join those of his enemies.

While such tactics succeeded to some extent in
creating a distorted image of Schnitzler's works,

the excellence of those works could not long remain obscured. As his fame spread, a number of his plays and short stories were translated into most of the major languages of Europe as well as into Hebrew, Japanese, and other tongues. Today his dramatic and narrative writings are widely acclaimed, and his thorough understanding of depth psychology is generally recognized.

On the other hand, his philosophical writings received little attention. Of these, his reflections on war and peace—prompted by and written during World War I—were not intended for publication. After Schnitzler's death. A partial compilation of these clearly pacifistic notes appeared in print. In 1967 these notes were published in a German edition of Schnitzler's aphoristic and essayistic writings (*Gesammelte Werke —Aphorismen und Betrachtungen,* Frankfurt). The English translation, prepared by me, is being published under the title *Some Day Peace Will Return: Notes on War and Peace* (New York: Frederick Ungar, 1971).

Two other philosophically oriented works were published in Schnitzler's lifetime: an extensive collection of aphorisms on a wide variety of subjects entitled *Reflections and Aphorisms (Buch der Sprüche und Bedenken),* and the original of the present text, *The Mind in Words and Actions (Der Geist im Wort und der Geist in der Tat).* Both publications, however, were issued in small printings and had not been translated when the barbaric book-burning by the Nazis destroyed most of the extant copies. Both these books, along with previously unpublished material, are now collected in the above-mentioned *Aphorismen und Betrachtungen,* which I edited. (A translation of *Buch der Sprüche und Bedenken* is being prepared.)

Schnitzler did not publish either of these two works until 1927. He may not have done so before because of his aversion to didacticism, which made him skeptical of all such writings, even his own. To be recognized as a philosopher was not one of his ambitions. On several occasions he expressed his pleasure at not having acquired disciples. Schnitzler's writings do not follow the form and organization of conventional philosophical works. Indeed, some professional philosophers may not recognize them as such because they do not readily fit into the main branches of contemporary philosophy. It is my opinion, however, that *The Mind in Words and Actions* does contribute to the phenomenology of ethics.

From whatever point of view Schnitzler's philosophical reflections may be evaluated, they all contribute to what is philosophy in its original and fundamental sense. Love of wisdom, the study of man's psychic nature, the examination of his relationship to his fellow men and of his cognition of himself—if these are legitimate objectives of philosophy, Schnitzler is certainly a philosopher.

The question of Schnitzler's total *Weltanschauung* has not yet been resolved. Some answers may be inferred from the content of this book, in conjunction with his other works, and additional answers may emerge if and when his diaries become available for study.

To those, however, who are acquainted with

Schnitzler's other works, it must already be
obvious that the principal objections previously
raised against Schnitzler's philosophy have no
substance: the assertions, namely, that he was
an absolute determinist, a relativist, an atheistic
materialist. Whenever the originators of such
erroneous statements bothered at all to "sub-
stantiate" them, they invariably quoted—usually
out of context—from Schnitzler's early publications.

It is quite true that, in his earlier years,
Arthur Schnitzler showed marked tendencies
toward a mechanistic concept of the world, as
well as an apparently all-pervading skepticism.
But it has been shown repeatedly that his views
underwent profound if gradual change. His later
works and statements prove conclusively that
the mature author postulated stable moral values
as indispensable to true humanity and that his
skepticism had mellowed to constitute little
more than an intellectual basis for scholarly
inquiry, a consistent admission of the ephemeral
nature of human knowledge, a prophylactic
against dogmatism.

We know, however, that over the years a
significant change in Schnitzler's philosophy did
occur, and this fact demonstrates two essential
aspects of his personality: flexibility, i.e., the
capacity for intellectual and spiritual growth;
and the element of incessant striving, the pursuit of a closer approximation to the truth, of a
more penetrating view of man and the world.

Since Schnitzler was, above all, a humanist, it
is perhaps more than chance that his only philosophical writings besides the aphorisms deal

with two of man's ever-acute problems: with war, man's principal bane, and with man's perpetual struggle to follow the ancient Pythic advice that is the key to all wisdom: *gnothi seauton* (know thyself).

There is even a causal relationship between the two problems. Both of them relate directly to the maturing of mankind. Between truly mature civilizations war is, by definition, impossible. Yet even at this moment, a major factor in the prevention of another world war is fear—the same emotion that so often in the past has functioned as a psychological catalyst in bringing wars about. Negotiations and agreements between antagonistic powers are of limited value, because the old adage that it takes two to make a fight does not necessarily hold true at this level, as historical events have shown. Only one force seems strong enough to dispel distrust and fear, the twin roots of war—enlightenment. Nothing short of realistic knowledge of his nature as an individual and of the nature of his species can help man to abandon his distrust and fear of others, in whom he senses—after all—a mirror image of himself. So long, however, as he is hampered in the emotional acceptance of such knowledge by aprioristic valuations, semantically anchored in prejudicial terminology, he will fail to gain much benefit from his self-study.

Whether or not Schnitzler's psychophilosophical categorization of the mind resulted from a conscious attempt to supply an instrument that might facilitate man's cognition of his mental structure remains an unanswerable question at this time. The important point is that he did create such an instrument. In the wrong hands, or rather in the wrong minds, it is all but useless. Superficial absorption of the text would either make the categorization sterile and academic or reduce it to the status of a parlor game for pseudointellectuals. Only accurate and full understanding of Schnitzler's thought can make it a meaningful and useful instrument.

In his analysis of the hidden causes of war and in his suggestions of steps toward its elimination (*Some Day Peace Will Return: Notes on War and Peace*), Schnitzler himself provided an example of the pragmatic applicability of *The Mind in Words and Actions*. Thus it is not cynicism that prompted him to base his suggestions on man's egoism rather than on lofty ideals or ethical considerations, but the grim realization that the majority of those who can be instrumental in deciding the issues of war and peace belong in the category of the *Un-menschen*, those people whose innate mentality renders them incapable of acting on vital matters from anything but self-interest.

Schnitzler's imaginative works have become part of world literature. They will be read by generations to come. Hopefully, so too will his philosophical legacy be given its rightful place.

The Mind in Words and Actions bears the subtitle *Preliminary Remarks Concerning Two Diagrams*. Since this has given rise to misunderstandings, it may be well to discuss briefly the nature of the work.

The entire text was considered by Schnitzler

primarily as a means of explaining the schematic drawings, but this view—though perhaps technically correct—does an injustice to the work, minimizing its importance by implication. Indeed, the first version of the original typescript is entitled "The Realm of the Mind, a Graphic Experiment" (*"Das Reich des Geistes, ein graphischer Versuch"*). One would probably do better to consider the diagrams as accessories to the text. They present a categorization of the intellectually oriented human mind as an abstract realm, characterized by hypothetical prototypes (i.e., pure types, not found in reality). The text without the diagrams can be understood by a careful reader; but the diagrams without the text would remain incomprehensible or be misunderstood.

If one attempts to classify this study in terms of conventional disciplines, one is at once confronted with the lack of a truly adequate terminology.

Since the study deals with the mind—although exclusively with the mind of intellectual man and with its manifestations in words and actions —one is tempted at first to consider it as belonging to psychology, especially in view of Schnitzler's great interest and competence in that field. This solution is unsatisfactory, however, because the work is not directly concerned with actual persons or groups.

With an occasional reservation that seems to pay tribute to Kantian conceptionalism, Schnitzler's ideal prototypes appear to be, at a first glance, pure ideas in the sense of Platonic "Extreme Realism," but the stipulated immanence of their essence within the individual finally marks them as the products of a philosophical approach closely related to Aristotelian "Moderate Realism." Are we dealing, then, with a philosophical work? Most philosophers would probably deny it, because the treatise in question does not fit into any of the principal branches of modern philosophy.

Nevertheless, in terms of its purpose the study serves one major aim common to both psychology and philosophy: to advance man's knowledge of himself.

In the eighteenth and early nineteenth centuries an appropriate term did exist: mental philosophy. It comprised both psychology and philosophy. Now, however, a new designation is needed. Although the coining of new words is generally unnecessary, such new terms are sometimes unavoidable for the sake of accuracy and therefore even desirable. Thus we may call Schnitzler's categorization of the mind a significant contribution to "psychophilosophy."

As for the subtitle, *Preliminary Remarks Concerning Two Diagrams,* the word "preliminary" does not mean that Schnitzler considered his study incomplete. He merely meant to emphasize that he did not claim permanent validity for his theory, that there is no finality about human cognitions, that whatever appears true today may be recognized as a fallacy tomorrow.

The purpose and scope of the work are best explained in Schnitzler's own brief prefatory remarks to the text.

Since *The Mind in Words and Actions* contains new concepts as well as transmutations of conventional terms, I have provided explanatory text notes.

My basic objective in this translation was to convey the ideas as Schnitzler expressed them, even at the occasional sacrifice of smoothness.

ROBERT O. WEISS

April 1971

THE MIND IN WORDS AND ACTIONS
Preliminary Remarks Concerning Two Diagrams

IN THE FOLLOWING PAGES an attempt is made to represent schematically in two diagrams the realm of the human mind insofar as it can manifest itself, first, by means of words, and secondly, by means of actions—especially the relationship between the prototypes of the human mind. No value judgment is intended hereby, but a categorization exclusively.

For many people, probably, this attempt will mean hardly more than a graphic game. On others, however, it may have a stimulating, in a certain sense even a reassuring, effect by resolving apparent contradictions that confuse us time and again in our evaluation of individuals because of the kind of form that these prototypes are compelled to take on in the world of phenomena.[1]

No claim is made for the completeness, much less for the final authoritativeness, of the explanatory remarks about these diagrams.

The Mind in Words

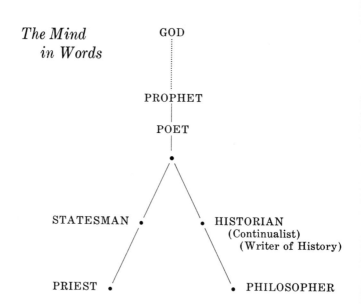

GOD

PROPHET

POET

STATESMAN   HISTORIAN
(Continualist)
(Writer of History)

PRIEST   PHILOSOPHER

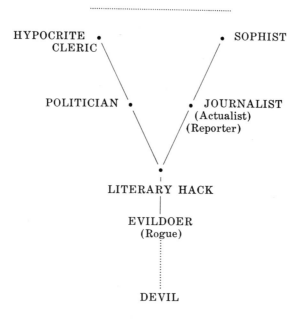

HYPOCRITE   SOPHIST
CLERIC

POLITICIAN   JOURNALIST
(Actualist)
(Reporter)

LITERARY HACK

EVILDOER
(Rogue)

DEVIL

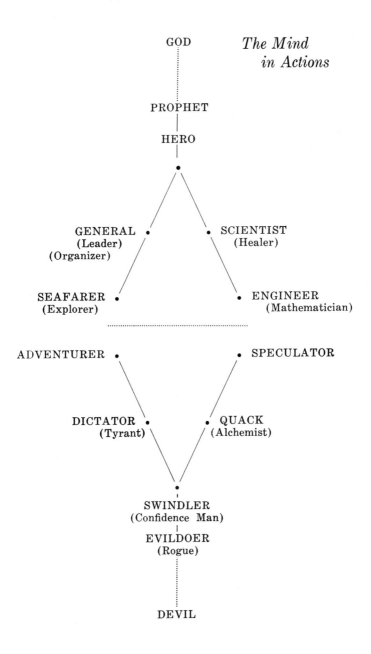

I
The Mind in Words

1

The Mind in Words diagram (like The Mind in Actions diagram) represents, as is evident, two appositive triangles with a common base.

The upper triangle represents the positive sphere of the human mind, aiming at the divine; the lower triangle represents the negative sphere, aiming at the diabolic, insofar as the mind is capable of manifesting itself by means of words.

The left side of the upper triangle ascends to the poet[2] from the priest by way of the statesman; the right side, from the philosopher by way of the historian (continualist).[3]

The left side of the lower triangle descends to the literary hack from the hypocrite cleric[4] by way of the politician; the right side, from the sophist by way of the journalist.

To designate the types the most striking words, not the most precise ones, were generally chosen. For better comprehension, however, variants have sometimes been added parenthetically to the diagram or they are merely mentioned in the text.

The absolutely precise word for the designation of the type exists in the language no more than this same type occurs in reality—and thus arbitrariness in nomenclature cannot be avoided entirely.

The designations applied here (priest, statesman, philosopher, historian, poet, hypocrite cleric, politician, sophist, journalist, literary hack) refer not at all to occupations or specific aptitudes, but to mentalities for which the corresponding specific aptitudes have a greater or lesser affinity, usually predisposing the representatives of the types concerned for the corresponding occupations.

Just as there is no intention of suggesting a spiritual or intellectual order of precedence among the prototypes through the rising and descending character of the sides of the triangle, no moral orientation of any kind is expressed either through the positioning on the right-hand or left-hand side. The words above and below, right and left, up and down, have merely graphic significance here, and the primary purpose of the arrangement of the types within the diagram is merely to determine the relationship of the types to each other.

Counter to each other at the corresponding points of the upper and the lower triangle are always placed those prototypes of mind between

which exist certain analogies of an external or
internal kind, analogies of such a compelling
nature that the representatives of the types concerned often seem to differ one from another
only because of their plus or minus signs—which
suffice, to be sure, to make them the most absolute opposites.

2

The borderline that separates the upper from
the lower triangle is conceptually impassable,
and every mentality as such is innate, integral,
and immutable. There are no transitions from
the positive types to the negative types, from humans, as we may call the representatives in the
upper triangle, to *Un-menschen*,[5] as we may
call the representatives in the lower triangle.

Neither are there any transitions from one
type to another in the same triangle. Occasionally we meet, of course, a philosophically inclined
statesman, a priestly poet, a historically minded
philosopher, a journalistically oriented politician, a sophist with the proclivities of a literary hack, etc., but close observation and, even
more, the experience of a good judge of human
nature, make it possible to diagnose with certainty the true nucleus, the original and integral
mentality, the prototype.

Whoever is born as a representative of the
type hypocrite cleric can never become a priest,
even if he chooses the calling of a priest. No
politician, even at the peak of his apparent
power, can ever develop into a statesman. No

literary hack, though endowed with the most dazzling gifts, has ever changed into a poet. It is logical then, that the sophist is worlds apart from the philosopher, the journalist (actualist),[6] from the historian, i.e., that these types are separated from each other by an impassable borderline.

But though the ideological borderline be impassable, the close yet deceptive and frequently tragic relationship between a type and its countertype—deceptive because they can so easily be mistaken for each other and sometimes tragic because of the unbridgeable abyss between them—precisely this relationship between type and countertype again and again disastrously brings about false diagnoses.

3

The difficulty, however, of distinguishing in every case the positive type from its countertype lies primarily in the fact that the representatives of the positive type are compelled—consciously or unconsciously—to adopt some of the modes of expression and ways of life of the corresponding negative countertypes. As a matter of fact, they are forced to disguise themselves, unintentionally or intentionally, as these countertypes whenever an impulse or an external necessity to act occurs.

Indeed, it could be said that a dash of the diabolical spirit is actually indispensable for the positive type, not only for its functioning but for its very existence.

Often enough the priest has to speak and conduct himself like a hypocrite cleric to be understood at all by the members of his congregation. Only seldom can the statesman do without the ways and means of the politician in order to attain a set goal. At times the philosopher resorts to the methods of the sophist so that he can lead his disciples by an easier path to the truth or to whatever seems to be the truth to him. In his presentations and lectures if in nothing else, the historian (continualist) cannot always completely avoid journalistic or sensational phraseology. Sometimes the poet seems to differ from the literary hack only by being less adept at having his efforts rewarded by the worldly success that frequently would constitute the very basis for his continued creative work.

It is this inevitability, indeed sometimes merely the anticipation of the inevitability, of not being able to do without that dash of the diabolical spirit that, under certain circumstances, makes for the tragic fate of such people. And the purer and higher the level on which they represent their type, the greater the danger that they perish from this tragedy.

On the other hand, however, there is innate in the negative type the striving, or at least a sometimes hardly conscious yearning, for the essence of his positive countertype. At times it is combined with the realization of the futility of such yearning. This may here also result in near-tragic conflicts that are, however, basically only tragicomical.

Still more frequently, the negative type tends either to feel, or at least to pose as, his cor-

responding positive countertype, though he real-
izes more or less clearly that his realm is
restricted to the negative sphere. In their
usurped roles such representatives of the negative type appear ridiculous, brazen, or pitiful—
depending on their aptitudes, their character
traits, and the environmental circumstances.
Sometimes, however, they succeed for a time,
by their adroitness, or perhaps their naiveté,
in deceiving even a good judge of human nature
as to their true nature.

Some representatives of the positive type are
condemned to walk the earth unrecognized as
long as they live, or even to be taken for their
corresponding countertypes. For others, a significant occasion is needed to elicit from them
what they really are. If such an occasion fails to
occur, it may happen that their own intrinsic
natures remain concealed from them all their
lives or poignantly reach their consciousness
only as faint intuitions.

Many a representative of the positive type
walks the earth intentionally disguised as his
countertype. Many a person, for a reason of his
own, enjoys acting permanently this role of a
countertype. Some keep on acting it out of re-
vulsion (despairing of mankind or despising it).
Frequently there occurs also a sort of mimicry
so that, for instance, many a statesman cannot
be distinguished—even by the experts—from the
swarm of politicians around him, or many a
priest from the hypocrite clerics. Now and then
it even happens that the positive type feels a
longing to be his countertype, inasmuch as he is
envious of the latter for his lightheartedness, for

his inner irresponsibility, and for the opportunities for greater effectiveness that occasionally are thereby increased.[7]

For a limited time—and, of course, always merely in appearance—a momentous occasion may transform a representative of the negative type into his positive countertype. Unusual times, a powerful personal experience, a great example, external pressure—all these may cause what seems to be such a transformation. Thus a politician with diplomatic, rhetorical, and organizational talents, for example, may on occasion appear like a statesman; an eloquent hypocrite cleric, like a priest; and, under the influence of a powerful personal experience, a literary hack may in one of his works give the impression of being a poet. But such deceit will never last long, and often the expert recognizes it the very moment it is attempted and succeeds with the masses.

4

The significance and the scope of a personality is by no means directly connected with its classification into the positive or negative sphere. There are persons of little aptitude and of negligible energy in the positive sphere, and there are persons of extraordinary vigor and great talents in the negative sphere. For the personality of the spiritual and intellectual man is determined not solely by his mentality but also by his aptitudes and *Seelenzustände*[8] (about which more will be said in the next chapter). In addition, his personality is determined, to a certain extent, by his outward appearance and physical characteristics insofar as the latter are influenced by *Seelenzustände* as well as by aptitudes, or inasmuch as, conversely, outward appearance and physical characteristics may affect *Seelenzustände*. There are, then, outstanding personalities even in the negative sphere, but great human beings exist only in the positive sphere, for only here can there be fruitfulness and continuity.

As a matter of fact, the general intellectual and cultural atmosphere is determined as much, or perhaps even to a greater extent, by the representatives of the negative type than by those of the positive type. The representative of the negative type exerts, not only through his accomplishments but also through his very being, an exciting, invigorating effect—though more often a disturbing one—to a higher degree than the representative of the positive type does. Only the latter, however, has a truly beneficial effect. Anything genuinely lasting is accomplished by the positive type only, in spite of the numerical preponderance of important personalities in the negative sphere.

The positive type, just as the negative one, is subject to error, but even his error is fruitful, for in his error there is still the truth of his personality. The positive type is ready at any time to give his life to his work. He is not interested in witnessing, as an individual, the victory of his work or of his idea. What is important to him is not personal posthumous fame but the immortality of his ideas.

The positive type is lonely, but integrated; the negative one is gregarious, but isolated.

Since he is working toward eternity and infinity, space is meaningless for the positive type. The negative type has no feeling for continuity. The past is dead for him, the future unimaginable; he can unfold in space only. He has "no time" in the true sense of the word, hence his impatience, his restlessness, and his unscrupulousness in the selection of his means.

5

It is in the nature of the priest and the statesman, i.e., the types on the left side of the triangle, to consider themselves the executors of a mission, perhaps of a divine task. A certain amount of intuition is characteristic of them and significant.

The philosopher and the historian, on the other hand, i.e., the types on the right side, are concerned with, and dependent on, facts and insights to a greater degree. They are furthered by doubts, while for the priest and the statesman doubts may, but do not have to, become dangerous.

It is possible to imagine a philosopher or a historian who lacks a streak of mysticism, but not a priest or a statesman. Yet, there are priests and statesmen who tend to be doubting or skeptical as well as philosophers and historians inclined to believe.

6

The priest wants devotion; the hypocrite cleric, submission; the statesman, growth; the politician, victory for his party (regardless of whether in the individual case this be progress or regression).

The philosopher seeks a higher order; the sophist, mere toying with ideas; the historian, insight and continuity; the journalist, speed and confusion; the poet, creativity and form; the literary hack, impressiveness and pleasing ornament.

Within the diagram, it is not fortuitous that the priest and the philosopher, even though on the same plane, are farthest apart from each other, and that the statesman and the historian —also on the same plane—are closer to each other than the priest and the philosopher.

By the same token it is significant that the priest and the hypocrite cleric, even though separated by the impassable line, as well as the philosopher and the sophist, are in closer proximity than the statesman to the politician on one side and the historian to the journalist on the other side, and that the literary hack and the poet are farthest apart from each other.

7

From the poet, i.e., from the apex of the upper triangle, an imaginary line leads to God by way of the prophet; from the literary hack, i.e., from the apex of the lower triangle, a line leads to the Devil by way of the evildoer.[9]

The prophet as well as the evildoer (rogue; for whose less pronounced manifestations, terms such as hoodlum or urchin suggest themselves) is in the same relative position in both The Mind in Actions and The Mind in Words[10] diagrams.

The representatives of these types, prophet and evildoer, reveal their nature quite often in the realm of delusion. And just as the prophet appears as a visionary and sometimes as one possessed, so the evildoer appears frequently as a rogue (especially in The Mind in Actions diagram).

There are, of course, no "representatives" for God and the Devil. They cannot be considered types at all. They are ultimate concepts; they are ideas to which appearance in earthly shape is denied.

8

There is a set of ethical concepts that assume validity, meaning, and reality only within the positive triangle, and a set of others that become valid, meaningful, and real only within the negative triangle. The individual components of these sets, the positive ones on one hand, the negative ones on the other, are in an unbridgeable contrast to each other, just as the positive and the negative types are.

The positive triangle represents the realm of truth, the negative one that of falsehood.

Similarly, in opposition to each other are the concepts of the divine[11] and the satanic, of altruism and egotism, of willingness to make sacrifices and inertia of the heart, of profound experience and mere thrill, of true vocation and pyramid-climbing, of worked-for fulfillment and the trappings of success, of humor and wit, of disinterested objectivity and opportunism, of pride and arrogance, of responsibility and frivolity, and still others.

Obviously, however, not every representative of the positive type is endowed with an affinity for all the ethical concepts characteristic of the positive sphere; nor does every representative of the negative type has an affinity for all concepts characteristic of the negative sphere. Thus, not every representative of the positive type exhibits divine characteristics or possesses humor, and not every representative of the negative type is satanically disposed or a liar by nature. This, however, is certain: that concepts characteristic of the negative sphere never play an essential part in the makeup of the positive prototypes, and concepts characteristic of the positive sphere never appear as essential aspects in the negative prototypes. In an individual case, for instance, a politician may not be lacking in a sense of responsibility, or a poet may appear frivolous in one of his works, but the concept of the totality of the personality is not disturbed hereby. In a higher sense, the hypocrite cleric, the politician, the sophist, the journalist, the literary hack have no traffic with truth and the other concepts in the positive set, while the priest, the statesman, the philosopher, the historian, and the poet have no traffic with falsehood and the other concepts in the negative set.

Most of these concepts and their strict appurtenance either to the positive or to the negative sphere require no explanation. The contrariety, for example, between altruism and egoism, between responsibility and frivolity, disinterested objectivity and opportunism, is immediately evident. For other contrasting concepts as, for instance, profound experience and mere thrill, true vocation and pyramid-climbing, something similar applies at times as was said regarding the contrariety of certain mentalities: that these concepts sometimes seem to be distinguished from each other only by their plus or minus signs. (For example, a fateful event that constitutes a profound experience for the poet is usually only a mere thrill to the literary hack, etc.) If, however, I look upon such concepts as the divine and the satanic (the quality of being divine and satanic), humor and wit (irony, satire), as absolute contrasts, and accept as a fact the exclusive affinity of the one set of concepts for the positive mentality, and that of the other set for the negative mentality, then an explanation is perhaps indicated.

That which gives the impression of the satanic in a person is a combination of base human qualities (malice, envy, hate) in an atmosphere of a more or less high intellectuality. That which appears divine is a combination of extraordinary intellectual gifts in the atmosphere of elevated *Seelenzustände*.

The satanic is always deliberate, intent on its

effect, and sterile, even while engaged in the
most lively activity. The divine is always un-
conscious, unconcerned with its momentary effect, and always fertile, even during a period of
what seems to be inaction.

The satanic, invariably, is only able to become
noticeable and to operate through its manifestations; the divine, simply by its existence.

Humor is always of a divine character. The
dominion of wit, irony, and satire, of these fallen
angels of the mind, is confined within the satanic.

To be sure, here too, an explanation—though
by no means a qualification—is necessary.
Which is that humor occasionally makes use of
irony, of satire, of wit for stylistic purposes;
that, quite frequently, a talent for satire, a
tendency of the spirit toward irony, a disposi-
tion toward wit, is found in representatives of
the positive type; that, as a matter of fact, a
great satirist may represent, according to his
mentality, the type of the philosopher, of the
historian, or even of the poet.

The principle then holds here too that an individual utterance, as well as a series of individual utterances, of a personality must be
recognized in terms of its ultimate motivation
and how these utterances are connected before
one may consider it a true characteristic of that
personality. And precisely because the total personality can hardly ever be fathomed as a whole,
the real comprehension of a personality, i.e.,
knowledge of human nature in the true sense of
the word, will ultimately always remain a matter
of intuition.

9

Since this diagram deals with prototypes of mentalities, any so-called definitions are automatically ruled out. I can attempt only descriptions, and they will probably . turn out to be nothing but casual characterizations of individual representatives of those prototypes.

Examples of the individual types probably suggest themselves at once to everyone, examples from history as well as from personal experience. Yet I am being careful not to adduce such examples. They would only confuse the matter since, after all, no individual can be completely representative of a prototype. This indicates a certain limitation to all humanity, but at the same time its inexhaustible plenitude.

In some cases, to be sure, the language usage itself so facilitates immediate comprehension that one may readily forgo an attempt at definitions or descriptions.

Thus the contrariety between priest and hypocrite cleric, philosopher and sophist, need not be illustrated at all. On the other hand, the politician will have appeared thus far, to some readers, as just a variant of, or perhaps as merely a lower form of, but not necessarily as the opposite of, the statesman. That such a contrariety exists between the literary hack (*Literat*) and the poet has probably become clear to larger segments of the population only within the last decades, through the common usage of those words. The total contrariety, however, that exists between the historian and the journalist, more correctly, between the continualist and the actualist—one so complete that we classify the former with the humans, the other with the *Un-menschen*—this contrariety will become clearer only through a few words of explanation to follow. [See No. 13.]

10

In the original sense of the term, the priest is one who administers the divine (religious, ritual) means of achieving grace. Yet this definition refers to the vocation, not to the mentality. As a type within our diagram he signifies helper, consoler, adviser, guide, friend. Of course, the sacerdotal vocation specifically authorizes a priest to dispense such means of achieving grace, regardless of whether one wishes to consider them of divine or of human origin. By no means, however, is it an indispensable prerequisite that the priest be pious in a religious or even in a dogmatic sense.

The hypocrite cleric (the designation *Pfaffe* took on its contemptuous connotation as early as the time of Luther) is in the same relationship to the priest—almost with the precision of an equation—as the politician to the statesman and the sophist to the philosopher.

It is just as natural that among the members of the sacerdotal vocation there are more hypocrite clerics than priests as that there are more politicians than statesmen among those people who enter government service. Numerically, the representatives of the negative type predominate among spiritually and intellectually oriented persons in a ratio that possibly corresponds to a biological law.

11

Heyne's German-language dictionary defines a statesman as a man "who knows how to direct matters of state, [one] to whom they are entrusted."

This somewhat casual definition is true of the prototype of the diagram only to a minor extent.

As is well known, matters of state are entrusted also to the politician, the negative type. It also cannot be denied that sometimes even the politician knows how to direct matters of state —just as the hypocrite cleric knows professionally how to deliver sermons and to hear confessions. The hypocrite cleric of any religion works for the advantage of his church—because the enlargement of its power signifies simultaneously an increase of his own power, or at least of his feeling of authority or of his fancied power. In the same way the politician promotes the interests of his party primarily from egoistic motives, even though he is sometimes not entirely conscious of them.

That well-known dictum that the end justifies the means holds as a rule of life for the politician as well as for the hypocrite cleric, indeed for all types in the negative sphere. In the positive sphere, however, the dictum holds that base means are capable of desecrating even the noblest end.

To the statesman, the welfare of his country is the supreme law. Yet he for whom the welfare of mankind rates higher than that of his own country, would have to be considered a statesman in the highest sense. Thus it will happen again and again that precisely the most genuine representatives of this type are held to be traitors in their own country, just as the noblest priests were persecuted, crucified, and burned as heretics.

Here it becomes most strikingly apparent that the more perfectly a representative of the positive type is characteristic of the prototype, the more readily he will be confronted with tragic conflicts.

12

In the real sense of the word, philosopher means a lover of wisdom.

As a prototype in the diagram, he denotes the thinker pure and simple, a person in whom the urge, the compulsion, the passion to think is innate. Language usage designates some people as philosophers, not because they are born thinkers, but because they view people, things, and conditions without emotional involvement or with resignation—an attitude toward the world and toward life that per se has nothing at all to do with philosophy.

The philosopher as a type in this diagram does not at all wish to arrive at so-called serenity. Primarily he wishes to attain to an inner clarity. He feels compelled to find the road to truth, even if he is convinced that the goal must remain unattainable.

To the sophist, the negative countertype, thinking is not a need and a passion but a game, one that, to be sure, may as such become a passion in turn. He is not an enemy of truth a priori, but even if he did consider it attainable, it would not constitute for him an ultimate goal worthy of pursuit. His only concern would be to entertain himself and others on the way to that goal, to impress and to dazzle. The iridescent paradox belongs to him above all, and for his purposes, according to the way in which he experiences life, truth and falsehood are indeed of equal value.

13

As to the prototype of the historian, the designation chosen corresponds least to the mentality it is intended to convey in the diagram. The type as such is not so much a historian, i.e., an investigator and writer of history, but rather someone with a feeling for history. He possesses a special gift for discerning causal relations, an intuition concerning the genesis of things; it is he who divines how things come into being. At the highest level he is the one who knows the continuity of past, present, and future: the continualist.

For most people history means a shadowy procession of ghosts acting out events for them, the outcome of which is known not only to the audience but also to the cast. But only he thinks truly historically who is able to experience in his mind past events as something happening in the present—and to do this in such a manner that he perceives the outcome of a process quite well known to him, while he reflects on its development, as something still uncertain for the time being, that he is really incapable of seeing it in any other way.[12]

But even though the historian as a prototype in the diagram does not stand for the historical investigator, the mentality [of the historian] naturally predisposes one to the profession of the historian.

An interest in causal relationships, a wide-awake sense of continuity, is generally a characteristic of all the positive types. In the historian (continualist), uncovering the connections between events in the more narrow and in the more extended sense, knowing the course of events, understanding their genesis, becomes a need, even a passion.

To the positive types this applies also with regard to their attitudes toward their own lives. They are always aware of the past and, as far as possible, of the future, while the existence of the negative types, as it were, consists of only a sequence of isolated moments. Yet, he who possesses only the present, possesses merely the moment, therefore in point of fact nothing.

By no means does the historian (continualist) have to occupy himself predominantly with the past. There are also historians of the present. The type remains the same—be he interested primarily in the Age of Reformation, or the French Revolution, or contemporary Spain.

The journalist as a type in the diagram—not the professional journalist—is characterized primarily by his interest in, and even his passion for, what is topical. The term actualist (not activist!), which immediately conveys his contrariety to the historian (continualist), would come closest to the essence of this mentality. He is entangled in matters of momentary interest, confused—even intoxicated—by what is happening day by day. In the depth of his soul, even the most significant event is a matter of indifference to the journalist unless it is at the same time topical or sensational. Conversely, the most insignificant matter assumes importance for him, if it is at the same time sensational or at least topical. Of all the representatives of the negative sphere, the representatives of this type are rooted most irrevocably in the immediate present. They know nothing about causal relationships, but only about some kind of [topical] references. All the characteristics of the negative type are most strongly expressed in this type. And nowhere is the intimate connection with the series of concepts that we have delineated as characteristic for the negative triangle so manifest as it is in the affinity of those concepts to the type of the journalist.

Eminent representatives of this negative type suffer especially frequently from the longing for the positive sphere; and they are fiercely hostile to it. Together with the politician and the speculator (whom we shall find in The Mind in Actions diagram), the type of the journalist represents the truly satanic element in the world.

Among the professional journalists there are

many who have few or none of the characteristics of the prototype, since journalism as a
vocation seems especially suited to harbor the
most diverse elements. On the other hand, it is
easy to understand that the mentality of journalism (sensationalism) predisposes its possessor
very distinctly to the vocation of the journalist.
One whom you would call a great journalist
hardly ever represents the prototype of the
journalist, but frequently, in terms of his mentality, the type of the historian (continualist),
sometimes the type of the statesman or the type
of the poet, occasionally also the type of the politician (a different type of the negative sphere,
then).

14

The poet is a maker and a preserver from
inner necessity. In his creative moments the entire world is to him material for his work. In his
unproductive ones the whole world loses for him
its luster or downright ceases to exist. No one
as much as he owes his creativity to the grace
of the moment.

He is the perpetual mirror of the world and
remains that, even when at times the mirror
clouds to the point of opacity.

To the literary hack the world is not, a priori,
material for his work. Rather, he is after topics.
He examines his experiences, his relationships,
his moods in terms of how he can perhaps use
and exploit them for his production. His experiences are for him, consciously or unconsciously,

means toward an end. He is incapable of confronting an experience, a person, a thing in a contemplative manner, i.e., with a truly pure heart. None of the negative types is ever so close to appearing tragic as he sometimes is, for he is the most conscious one among them. But in any case, he remains merely a tragicomical figure, even though frequently one of considerable stature.

Of all types he is the most *un-menschlich*. Therefore he is properly to be described as satanic even in his most eminent forms, although he is occasionally credited with [having something of] "the divine."

In the poet, the path of life and that of creativity are one and the same. In the literary hack they are two paths that—at certain elevated moments—may run close to each other, may even merge so completely that the impression of one single path is created and the literary hack is taken for a poet. The type of the literary hack is by no means to be found exclusively among writers. Many people who have nothing to do with the trade of the literary hack demonstrate the literary hack's attitude toward life in the sense that they are always concerned with observing themselves, that they have a tendency to admire themselves narcissistically while neglecting their basic responsibilities, sometimes even to their own detriment.

The poet always gives himself, even in a work in which he is fatigued and inadequate. The literary hack preserves himself, even when he seems to squander himself. The quantitative preponderance of the negative principle in the world is shown here even more clearly than elsewhere: there are many more renowned literary hacks than there are renowned poets. But no literary hack, even though he may have created master-pieces, has ever been a great human being.

II

An Inserted Chapter
on Aptitudes
and Seelenzustände

1

At first glance it may seem as if not all
posited mentalities that are possible within this
diagram have been included with the types set
forth. Some will look in vain for the satirist,
the dilettante, the critic, the melancholiac, the
fanatic, the skeptic, the enthusiast, as well as
many others.

These above-named types and many others
will not be found in the diagram simply because
they do not belong in it. For the critic, enthusiast, skeptic, etc., absolutely never represent the prototype of a mentality. All these and
other terms that might seem to belong in the
diagram pertain not to mentalities but to aptitudes and *Seelenzustände*, which in a similar
way contribute in a lesser or higher degree to
conditioning and determining the personality
of intellectual man.

2

Absolutely firm, immutable relationships are not postulated, yet undoubtedly a certain affinity —rather far from being a natural law—does exist between certain mentalities and certain aptitudes, exists more rarely between certain mentalities and certain *Seelenzustände,* and exists hardly ever between certain aptitudes and certain *Seelenzustände.* A certain mentality is at times the prerequisite for the existence of certain aptitudes and of certain *Seelenzustände.* The reverse is never the case.

While the mentalities always represent something given a priori, something stable, unified, and essential, and therefore unalterable, this criterion of immutability by no means applies in the same measure and to the same extent to the *Seelenzustände* or even to the aptitudes.

It is not improbable that the mentalities are subject to definite, anatomic-histological conditions. That is probably also true—to a degree difficult to determine—for the aptitudes, especially for the specific aptitudes. The *Seelenzustände,* however—not only the floating ones[13] but also those that are apparently stable, such as character traits, dispositions, qualities—are, most likely, determined by physiochemical processes, perhaps chiefly by endocrine ones of either a regular or a fluctuating nature, toward which a propensity is usually innate.[14]

Of course, neither the mentalities nor the aptitudes nor the *Seelenzustände* are materially explained by postulating such purely physiological functions. The intention is merely to indicate an undoubtedly existing relationship between mentalities, aptitudes, and *Seelenzustände* on one side and their physical correlates on the other—a relationship whose nature is by no means obvious (and perhaps does not always indicate dependence). Even if we were to succeed in localizing with certainty a mentality (or perhaps a specific aptitude) at a definite place in the brain or to establish a causal relationship between a *Seelenzustand* and the function of a certain nerve or a certain gland, the real nature of the spirit and the soul would remain just as incomprehensible as before (just as the actuality of eyesight as such is by no means explained by the fact that the ability to see depends on the existence and proper functioning of the optic nerve).

3

We can distinguish general and specific aptitudes.

The general aptitudes could also be called general predispositions of an intellectual kind as, for instance, industry, imagination, sagacity, in contrast to the predispositions of an ethical kind, the true tendencies of character as, for example, kindness, justice, cruelty, etc.

With some general traits it is difficult to decide whether they are to be classified with intellectual traits rather than with traits of an ethical nature (as, for instance, slyness).

In terms of the total personality, the general aptitudes are often more significant than the specific aptitudes and, depending on their strength, also more or less decisive for the possibilities of development of a specific aptitude. Thus imagination, for example, will have a furthering effect upon poetic aptitude, sagacity upon philosophic aptitude, etc.

A general aptitude must not be confused with aptitudes in a number of fields, which is usually understood as the occurrence of several specific aptitudes in one and the same individual.

Certain of the general aptitudes show—just as certain of the specific aptitudes do—an affinity for a certain mentality. Thus the so-called diplomatic aptitude will be found particularly often in the statesman and the politician.

At this point, only the poetic aptitude as well as the literary, the rhetorical, the diplomatic, and the political ones are mentioned as examples representative of a hundred other specific aptitudes.

One notices here, not for the first time, that the same designations are used for some kinds of specific aptitudes as are applied to the types of mentalities. And precisely the fact that the word for a certain specific aptitude and for a certain mentality is frequently identical often provides the cause for grave errors and erroneous judgments. Poetic mentality, however, and poetic aptitude, journalistic mentality and journalistic aptitude, etc., are by no means the same, and—like mentalities and vocations—mentalities and aptitudes must be strictly differentiated, even when the same term is used for both.

Though the specific aptitudes are really innate, they need by no means develop in every case; indeed, they need not even ever emerge. Environmental influences, one's destiny, may cause them either to be stunted or to fully develop. A mentality as such, however, can neither atrophy nor be perfected.

Certain affinities between certain mentalities and certain aptitudes are immediately evident as, for instance, that between the poetic mentality and a specific poetic aptitude. Yet here, too, it is always only a matter of an affinity, not of a necessary linking, let alone of mentality and aptitude being the same thing. On occasion one may find a very large amount of poetic aptitude though the individual in question is not a representative of the prototype of the poet, just as, on the other hand, we meet genuine representatives of the prototype of the poet with little poetic aptitude.

Thus there are writers with great poetic aptitude who, according to their mentality, should be designated not as poets but as historians (continualists). There are also poetic aptitudes (especially those with a predominantly psychological orientation) that—according to their mentality—belong to the type of the scientist[15] (see The Mind in Actions diagram), and there are poets, sometimes of a higher order, who are to be classified with the type of the prophet.

The affinities between certain mentalities and kindred aptitudes are more evident and more strongly expressed in the negative sphere than in the positive sphere. For example, there are representatives of the prototype of the statesman with meager diplomatic aptitude and representatives of the prototype of the politician with great political talent. Thus it may happen that the highly gifted politician is taken for a great statesman, and a meagerly gifted statesman for an inferior politician.

Every kind of aptitude can be found in the types of the positive sphere as well as in those of the negative sphere.

The more pronounced the affinity is between the innate mentality and the specific aptitude and the better this specific aptitude is developed, the more substantial, generally speaking, the individual intellectual accomplishment is.

It need not be pointed out that a whole series of aptitudes—the aptitude for music, for example—do not belong in these expositions, which are concerned only with the mind as reflected in words and with the mind as reflected in actions. But of course, among the musicians are men of intellect, i.e., representatives of a mentality, just as, often enough, we find people, even among the members of the so-called intellectual professions, who cannot be classified as men of intellect.

4

The *Seelenzustände* are divided into character traits which the temperaments are a part of, psychological qualities, flowing *Seelenzustände,* and moods. And by this sequence there is simultaneously indicated, in descending order, the degree of their variability and the measure of their importance for the total personality. Abso-

lute immutability, however, which is a characteristic of a mentality, can never be claimed for the
Seelenzustände, nor even for the character
traits, even though their relative variability becomes apparent or gains practical importance
only in exceptional cases.

That absolute immutability may not even be
claimed for the character traits may perhaps be
proved by the fact that in certain diseases of
the brain (e.g., paretic neurosyphilis) a first
symptom—not always interpreted correctly at
once—is noted: a change of character, indeed
where character seems to be transformed into
its exact opposite. (On occasion, for example, a
mild, prudent person changes into an irascible,
vicious one, or a miser turns into a spendthrift.)
A mentality, to be sure, may be destroyed by a
cerebral disease, but it can never be transformed
into another mentality. No sophist has ever become a philosopher through cerebral disease;
no priest has thus become a hypocrite cleric; no
continualist an actualist; etc.

At this point the fact may be mentioned that
in extremely rare cases a trauma, for instance
a blow on the head, is said to have actually
caused the development of a specific aptitude,
especially a musical one—or rather that the
aptitude is supposed to have emerged only under
the influence of such a trauma.

Even where one cannot precisely speak of
variability, the character traits can be influenced not only by environmental factors but
also by internal processes. (This is least true of
the so-called temperaments.) A character trait
continues to develop or regresses, but in either

case a person's own will may participate in the process, which—to be sure—in turn constitutes a character trait in its own right.

Flowing *Seelenzustände* are those that usually not only change in terms of intensity and duration but also show a tendency to disappear temporarily or permanently or—under the influence of certain experiences—to change into their real or seeming opposite.

One would like to assume a priori of certain character traits that they can be found exclusively in the representatives of the positive types or exclusively in the representatives of the negative types in the same way that we were justified in assuming such exclusiveness for certain concepts—in the same way, then, that we recognized, for instance, that truth, the divine element, the spirit of sacrifice, profound experience, etc., pertain exclusively to the positive type, and that the lie, the satanic element, egoism, sensationalism, etc., exclusively to the negative type. To make this assumption, however, would be an error. There is hardly any character trait whose occurrence is restricted to the representatives of the positive prototype or to the representatives of the negative prototype.

Nevertheless, there are affinities between certain mentalities and certain character traits. Thus a priestly mentality, for example, can hardly be imagined without goodness, a trait that we shall meet rather frequently in the types of the positive sphere. But in the types of the negative sphere we shall probably never meet true goodness, though often enough we encounter the good-naturedness that is so frequently confused with it and usually signifies nothing but weakness.

The qualities assume an intermediate position between the traits and the flowing *Seelenzustände,* and it is a question whether we should consider, or be justified in considering, them *Seelenzustände* sui generis.

It cannot by any means always be easily decided whether some psychological quality is to be considered a character trait or a flowing *Seelenzustand* in a narrower sense, or whether, in a given instance, we are confronted with a flowing *Seelenzustand* or with a mood. The differentiation is that much more difficult because a flowing *Seelenzustand* may gradually develop into a quality (e.g., suspicion, bitterness) and because, through frequent recurrence, a mood may acquire the significance of a flowing *Seelenzustand,* perhaps even of a quality.

Qualities that we encounter more frequently as character traits among the types of the positive sphere usually appear merely as moods or flowing *Seelenzustände* among the types of the negative sphere.

When a trait or a quality or a flowing *Seelenzustand* within a personality structure plays a dominant part, we like to use the adjective describing this trait, this quality, this *Seelenzustand,* in connection with the word "nature." We refer then, for example, to people of enthusiastic, dilettante, fanatic, and other natures.

A truly enthusiastic nature, for example, probably exists only among the positive types. Occasional enthusiastic moods exist often enough among the negative types (perhaps under the influence of mass suggestion).

On the other hand, some psychological attributes (qualities) that frequently are considered original character traits should very often be evaluated merely as flowing *Seelenzustände.*

Bravery and cowardice, for instance, are original character traits much more rarely than one may think. There are few born cowards and even fewer born heroes.

Neither do faith and skepticism occur very often as character traits. Indeed they are flowing *Seelenzustände par excellence,* and frequently even they occur only as moods. How could one understand otherwise the fact that even devout natures often become doubtful of their God— and that again and again skeptics are converted to a creed or quite generally to belief.

Within the same human soul a certain quality may be present simultaneously as aptitude, as character trait, and as a flowing *Seelenzustand.* Sometimes there occurs, for example, an aptitude for criticism combined with a kind of a criticistic character trait (passion for fault-finding). Often enough such a trait exists without a specific aptitude for criticism. Conversely, an aptitude for criticism frequently exists without a real criticistic character trait.

The *Seelenzustand* of fault-finding will be observable especially often among the representatives of the negative types. Especially here—as a flowing *Seelenzustand*—it tends to develop into a quality, since it usually evolves from feelings of inferiority, vanity, and resentment. Politicians, journalists, literary hacks are primarily disposed toward the *Seelenzustand* of fault-finding.

One might think that the tendency toward the *Seelenzustände* of dilettantism is to be expected only among the negative types, but precisely this *Seelenzustand,* as a trait as well a flowing *Seelenzustand,* is by no means rare among the positive types.

The designation of dilettantism, after all, pertains to those whom colloquial usage usually deals with most arbitrarily. Sometimes one designates as a dilettante an artist of a certain aristocratic inner style of life, a playfully disposed intellect who is less interested in the perfection of a work than in the enjoyment of creativity or play per se. Then one sometimes applies that term to a modestly gifted individual who ventures to undertake tasks to which he is unequal and who appears pitiful or ridiculous because of his unfounded ambitions.

Dilettantism as a *Seelenzustand* has nothing to do with the extent of one's aptitude.

Literary hacks are less subject to the *Seelenzustand* of dilettantism (and also must be more on their guard against it) than poets. There is a kind of dilettantism for which one might consider as the proper designation the word mattoidism (taken from the field of psychopathology and little known among the laity), a condition that can be briefly characterized as a combination of feeblemindedness and of some kind of a specific, usually artistic aptitude, in varying proportions. There are mattoids who, on occasion, give the impression of possessing bizarre talents. Others (or the same ones at different times) give the impression of being dullards or fools.

There are poets of a high order who were dilettantishly oriented during periods of their existence or in reference to one work or another. And there are also poets, not only literary hacks with poetic aptitude, who show an undoubtedly mattoid trait. (Some of the so-called unrecognized geniuses belong in this category.)

The *Seelenzustand* of feuilletonism (in contrast to that of dilettantism) belongs to those who demonstrate an affinity probably to only the types of the negative sphere. Actually, there does exist an especially strong affinity of the *Seelenzustand* of feuilletonism to the mentality of journalism.

The characteristics of the feuilletonistic *Seelenzustand* are: lack of a feeling of responsibility, indifference toward that which is essential, indifference to facts, superficiality. All this combined with a specific literary aptitude naturally predisposes one for using, or as the case may be, mastering, the artistic medium that we call the feuilleton. There are feuilletonists by profession, but there are also feuilletonists of aptitude who are (sometimes to their detriment) by no means feuilletonists according to their *Seelenzustände*.

There is, of course, no specifically dilettante aptitude. There are only specific aptitudes of some kind in combination with a dilettante trait or with a dilettante *Seelenzustand*. (One can choose the profession of a feuilletonist, but not the profession of a dilettante.)

As moods we designate *Seelenzustände* that

are the most dependent on external influences
and are of a relatively transitory nature, such as
gaiety, peevishness, anger, etc. Moods that recur
frequently, even without an evident or sufficient
external cause, suggest an existing trait. Often
enough, under the influence of circumstances, a
mood gradually develops beyond a flowing
Seelenzustand into a quality that becomes in-
eradicable and functions like a character trait,
attaining the same significance. The possibility
for such a development exists more often for
moods of a negative kind than for those of a
positive kind. Out of frequently recurring moods
of being aggrieved, of bitterness, of rancor, the
corresponding flowing *Seelenzustände* (for instance, bitterness) or qualities (for instance,
distrust) develop more readily than a series of
pleasurable and gay moods evolves into a
permanent condition of cheerfulness.

5

There was no intention at all to venture by
these cursory remarks a systematization of aptitudes and of *Seelenzustände*. What mattered
here was only to make evident, through individual examples, the relationship and affinities
that exist conceptually and actually between the
mentalities on one side and the aptitudes and
Seelenzustände on the other, and to emphasize
how necessary it seems to be to keep separate
the mentalities on the one hand and the aptitudes
and *Seelenzustände* on the other, in order to be
able to grasp accurately the innermost nature of

a personality and to identify the innate, uni-form, unchangeable prototype as such.

Generally the personality of men of intellect as such is determined by his mentality, aptitudes (general and specific), *Seelenzustände* (charac-ter traits, flowing *Seelenzustände,* and moods), and, to a lesser degree, by external appearance and physical properties. The uniqueness of a personality, however, is determined: first, by the degree to which each of these elements is present within that personality; secondly, by the relationship of these elements to each other; and third, by something incommensurable that we may perhaps designate as the divine or, as the case may be, the diabolic, be it in a religious or in a philosophical sense.

Yet this incommensurable element in a per-sonality is presumably that same unique rela-tionship of these elements to each other that appears only and exclusively in that particular personality.

III
The Mind in Actions

1

In all its details and in its basic idea The Mind
in Actions diagram is an exact counterpart to
The Mind in Words diagram.

Here, too, it is a matter of two appositive
triangles that are separated from each other by
a common base.

Here, too, the upper triangle represents the
positive sphere, oriented in the direction of
the divine, and the lower triangle represents the
negative sphere, oriented in the direction of the
diabolic. Within these spheres the mind's activity operates—here, however, not insofar as
the mind can manifest itself by means of words
but insofar as it can do so by actions.

The general rules referring to The Mind in
Words diagram retain their validity also in re-
spect to The Mind in Actions diagram. Therefore:

The borderline that separates the upper and the lower triangle from each other is conceptually impassable.

Every mentality as such is uniform and unchangeable.

There exists a profound, a deceptive, and, not rarely, a tragic relationship between a type and the corresponding countertype.

A dash of the diabolic spirit is actually indispensable for the positive type, not only for its functioning but for its very existence.

Thus the relationship between type and countertype is here absolutely analogous to the relationship of type and countertype in The Mind in Words diagram. But the representatives of the types in question are more rarely conscious of this relationship than the types of The Mind in Words diagram, and hardly ever to the same extent.

2

Again, the absolutely precise terms for the types of The Mind in Actions diagram are hardly to be found, and here, too—just as in The Mind in Words diagram—I have selected as memorable a word as possible, not necessarily the most apt term.

The difficulty of finding absolutely precise terms for the types of this diagram is partially caused by the fact that conceptually—if at all—actions are still harder to comprehend than words, because we are here confronted with an almost unlimited number of possibilities.

In The Mind in Actions diagram we are concerned never with types of occupations or with aptitudes, but with types of mentalities. To be sure, the innate mentality here also predisposes the individual for the occupation with which it shares its designation. Yet the external or inner necessity for the individual representative of a given type of mentality to choose the occupation designated by the analogous word is still less compelling than in The Mind in Words diagram.

3

The following are the types in The Mind in Actions diagram.

On one side (the left) of the positive triangle, a straight line ascends from the seafarer (explorer) to the hero by way of the general (leader, organizer).

On the other (right) side the line ascends from the engineer (mathematician) once again to the hero, by way of the scientist (healer).

And just as in The Mind in Words diagram, we find in the negative triangle the corresponding negative countertypes in an analogous arrangement.

The left side of the negative triangle descends to the swindler from the adventurer by way of the dictator, the right side, from the speculator by way of the quack.

Thus we have the adventurer as the countertype to the seafarer, the dictator to the leader, the speculator to the engineer, the quack to the scientist, the swindler to the hero.

In this diagram, even more so than in the preceding one, variants, in addition to the main designations that we have chosen for the prototypes, obtrude upon the mind at once. Which designation we should prefer in an individual case for the representative of a certain mentality often depends on the aptitudes and the *Seelenzustände*. Thus for many a representative of the type of the adventurer, especially for those on a lower ethical and intellectual level, a designation such as *commis voyageur*[16] may be preferable.

Sometimes the designation tyrant might seem more suitable than dictator. I have chosen the word dictator for the main designation primarily because the representatives of this type are by no means always tyrannical—not even in terms of their character traits. Rather, they are pedantic, harsh, and cruel, while it is precisely the general (leader, organizer), i.e., the positive countertype of the dictator, who frequently appears to be—and on occasion really is—tyrannical when necessity requires it. For inferior representatives of the prototype of the dictator more banal terms, such as drill sergeant, come to mind.

Depending on the contingencies, some representatives of the type of the speculator could be called operators, gamblers, crooks, and, under certain circumstances, perhaps fantasts.

In the place of quack, now the designation alchemist, now the designation poison peddler may seem appropriate.

The type of the swindler confronts us sometimes as a confidence man and occasionally also in the guise of a fool, a prankster, a clown.

Just as in The Mind in Words diagram, an imaginary line leads from the apex of the positive triangle to God by way of the prophet. Another imaginary line leads from the apex of the negative triangle to the Devil by way of the evildoer (rogue).

Thus the prophet and the evildoer, just as God and the Devil, are related in the same manner in The Mind in Words diagram as in The Mind in Actions diagram.

4

This is not the only way in which a relationship—one may say, as if dictated by a natural law—is expressed between the two diagrams, The Mind in Words and The Mind in Actions.

For if we compare the two diagrams, we recognize the fact that certain analogies, psychological relationships of a lesser or greater degree, exist also between the prototypes located at analogous points in both diagrams, so that sometimes one diagram appears like a confirmation or a justification of the other.

Just as in The Mind in Words diagram, intuition as well as faith in a cause seems to be characteristic of and significant for one side, the left. For the other, the right side, the spirit of inquiry, the drive for knowledge and for accumulating facts seem to be characteristic and significant.

The priest and the statesman are in need of intuition and faith more than the philosopher and the historian, while the latter have to rely on as great a measure of knowledge as possible to fulfill the purpose of their mentality. In the same way the seafarer (explorer) and the general (leader, organizer) rely on their inner voice, perhaps on their guiding star, more confidently than the engineer (mathematician) and the scientist, for whom accumulating knowledge, organizing, and drawing comparisons are prerequisites for being efficacious, indeed for possessing the feeling of being fulfilled.

Of course, the usefulness of knowledge and insights for the types of the other side is equally unquestionable. Nevertheless, it is easier to imagine the seafarer (explorer) and also the general (leader, organizer) without a great amount of knowledge and insights, indeed even without any special desire for them, than it is to imagine the engineer (mathematician) without the necessary technical training or the scientist without the necessary wealth of observations and the need to gather ever new ones.

5

The relationship of the negative to the positive types in The Mind in Actions diagram corresponds to the relationships in The Mind in Words diagram.

Thus the adventurer is the negative countertype, occasionally even the caricature, of the seafarer (explorer), just as in The Mind in Words diagram the hypocrite cleric represents the negative countertype of the priest.

Furthermore, the dictator (tyrant) is related to the general as the politician is to the statesman.

The speculator is related to the engineer as the sophist is to the philosopher.

The quack is related to the scientist (healer) as the journalist (actualist) is to the historian (continualist).

The swindler (confidence man) is related to the hero as the literary hack is to the poet.

Not only the everyday use of the language but also certain metaphors sometimes express the relationships suggested here in a surprising and revealing manner.

Occasionally one can quite aptly describe the sophist—who occupies the same position in The Mind in Words diagram as the speculator in The Mind in Actions diagram—as a "speculator" in words. One can also describe the journalist (actualist), who in The Mind in Words diagram occupies the same position as the quack in The Mind in Actions diagram, as a "quack" of public opinion; and the literary hack, who in The Mind in Words diagram occupies the same position as the confidence man in The Mind in Actions diagram, as a "confidence man" of the intellect.

The hero and the poet are akin to each other in the realm of the spirit (a poet without intellectual courage is as inconceivable as a hero without physical courage), in the same way that the swindler is akin to the literary hack. As a matter of fact, regardless of the strictest circumscription of a category, relationships of varying degrees can be demonstrated again and again between the different types. And in general, the relationship between the types located at corresponding points of the two diagrams seems to be a closer one than that between the types within the same diagram.

Thus the spiritual relationship between the type of the mathematician and that of the philosopher is a closer one than that between the mathematician and the scientist or the philosopher and the historian. The relationship between the general (organizer, leader) and the statesman is a more intrinsic one than that between the statesman and the priest, etc.

6

To the casual judge many a type will seem to be still missing from the mentalities that I have assembled in the two diagrams, e.g., the jurist, the economist, the physicist, the chemist, the architect, the inventor, etc. Here, as is true of many other examples, it is not at all a question of prototypes of mentalities but of designations of types of occupations or aptitudes that may—but do not have to—have a propensity for certain mentalities, so long as it is a question of a man of intellect in an individual case under consideration.

For not everyone in the so-called intellectual occupations, not even every intellectually gifted person, can be designated as a man of intellect according to our definition of the term. To be such a man of intellect, one must have above all an innate mentality, one that is, as we know, in every case uniform and immutable. Consequently, there are some jurists, writers, physicians, theologians, and, to be sure, even professors of philosophy, just as there are economists, industrialists, and businessmen, whom one can by no means consider real men of intellect.

Yet, even though the jurist, for example, as a specific type, must be omitted from our diagram because there is no specific juridical mentality, there are, nevertheless, a few mentalities that the jurist (i.e., the lawyer, the legal scholar, the judge) may represent. Some legal scholars represent the type of the philosopher; others represent the type of the historian. Some lawyers represent the type of the sophist or of the literary hack, just as there are physicians who—according to their mentalities—are to be classified neither with the scientists nor with the quacks but with the priests.

Many an industrialist—according to his mentality—has to be classified with the planners, many an economist with the statesmen, philosophers, politicians. As a man of the intellect, the physicist as well as the chemist has to be classified sometimes with the type of the mathematician, sometimes with the type of the scientist. The architect, the technologist, usually has to be classified with the type of the mathematician (engineer). The businessman as a man of intellect may represent the type of the speculator or of the politician, and, in special cases, also the type of the statesman. We may meet the inventor as the type of the mathematician, of the scientist, of the speculator (schemer), perhaps even of the poet.

The essential element, however, for judging

and recognizing the man of intellect and decisive for the role he is assigned in the intellectual and spiritual history of mankind—whether
he participate through words or through actions, whether as a positive or as a negative
type—is not the occupation, not the aptitude,
not even the *Seelenzustände*. The essential element is always the innate, uniform, and unchangeable mentality that he represents in the
world of phenomena, even though it is especially
the mentality—being the deepest element of the
personality—that can hide from the inspection
of even a good judge of human nature for a
shorter or longer time, or even that, in rare
cases, reveals itself only in historical retrospect.

Translator's Notes

[1] The word phenomena is to be understood in its original philosophical meaning: physical or sensual appearances (as opposed to noumena, the conceptual essences, or *abstracta*, of Platonic idealism). Here Schnitzler seems to approach closely a Kantian type of conceptualism that restricts the area of rational methods to the phenomenon and holds that the noumenon (*das Ding an sich*) can be comprehended only through intuitive processes.

[2] In line with the German *Dichter* the expression does not mean here lyrical poet but applies also to great prose writers.

[3] As a parenthetical alternate for historian, Schnitzler offers the word *Kontinualist*. The term indicates here someone who sees events not as isolated occurrences but in their causal relationship. He is one who recognizes, e.g., the organic continuity of history and will, therefore, more rarely misjudge the relative importance of any given event in the past or in the present. Because it is untranslatable, I have used the word continualist.

[4] The German word is *Pfaffe,* for which there is no exact English equivalent. Originally meaning "priest," *Pfaffe* is now a derogatory or contemptuous term. While a militant atheist might apply the term indiscriminately to all clergymen, even a religious person might apply it to a clergyman of his own faith, if he were convinced of the latter's dishonesty, hypocrisy, or incompetence.

[5] By hyphenating the German word *Unmensch* (which means a brutish or monstrous person), Schnitzler gives the word this meaning: a man not governed by his better nature.

[6] *Aktualist,* the parenthetical alternate for the term journalist, has no exact English equivalent. It is descriptive of someone who looks at events only as separate, isolated occurrences and who, therefore, evaluates them exclusively in terms of their momentary impact. Thus he frequently misjudges the true (historical) importance of contemporary events. He prefers news to truth. We shall use in this text the word actualist.

[7] That is to say, the increase may be effected by a lack of moral responsibility. That this may result in greater "freedom" of action is obvious. Thus it is not the inner irresponsibility that the positive type may envy, but the opportunity for increased effectiveness.

[8] Literally: "conditions of the soul." See No. 2 in Chapter II. The singular is *Seelenzustand.*

[9] The term evildoer (Schnitzler used *Tücke-bold*) is to be understood here as designating the greatest concentration of evil in human form, i.e., a relatively "pure" manifestation thereof, while the rogue (Schnitzler used *Bösewicht*)—

suggested as an alternate for evildoer in the diagram itself—may embody evil in its psycho-pathological incarnations, such as power-mad dictators, psychopaths in general, etc.

[10] That is to say, these two types are farthest apart from each other and occupy the same relative position, at the apex of their respective triangles.

[11] Schnitzler gives the words *Dämonie* and *dämonisch* a meaning deviating from the customary usage of these words. He contrasts the realm of the satanic, which stands for the evil, the negative, the diabolic, with what, for the lack of a more adequate term, I have translated by "divine," designating the good, the positive, the beneficial.

[12] Among the discussions of the functions of history and the historians, Friedrich Nietzsche's "On the Usefulness and Disadvantages of History" (*Vom Nutzen und Nachteil der Historie für das Leben*, 1873–1874) is of special interest here because it invites comparison with Schnitzler's views. The same historical sense, the empathic capability of living the past, as it were, so highly valued by Schnitzler, is decried by Nietzsche as a paralyzing factor that deprives its possessor of initiative, of the desire to act independently of the past, of his ability to build for the future. While Nietzsche admits the usefulness of "monumental history," which provides inspiration and strength to act from only the great accomplishments of the past, he rejects "antiquarian history" and "critical history." The former is rejected chiefly because of its tendency to hide behind the past and to venerate

the present as a sacrosanct result of past glories; the latter, because it attempts, through criticism and judgment of the past, to eliminate a part of the historic reality and thus achieve a synthetic better present. Here the disparity between the views of Schnitzler and those of Nietzsche may be more seeming than real, since the character- istics of Nietzsche's "antiquarian historian" and "critical historian" are such that they would fit readily into Schnitzler's "negative sphere," that their prototype would be that of the "journalist" rather than that of the "historian." Nietzsche's "monumental historian," on the other hand, is not drawn distinctly enough for classification within Schnitzler's diagrams. He could be a representative of the statesman, the historian, or the leader, as easily as of the politician, the journalist, or the dictator. There is no doubt, however, that Schnitzler's concepts are generally in agreement with Nietzsche's scathing denun- ciation of the Hegelian school of history (in the same essay). Still, one must keep in mind the fact that Nietzsche and Schnitzler approach the historian from different viewpoints: Nietzsche deals with an intellectual problem, Schnitzler analyzes a prototypal mentality.

[13] The original text reads *fließende Seelen- zustände,* i.e., psychic conditions that are subject to change—but the changes are smooth transi- tions, not abrupt ones as in changing moods.

[14] Schnitzler's assumption that mentalities and aptitudes may have an anatomic-histological foundation is shared by a number of scientists but has not yet been proved conclusively. The related, though by no means identical theories of

E. Kretschmer (*Physique and Character*, New York, 1925), for example—with which Schnitzler may have been acquainted—seem to have found little confirmation by other investigators. On the other hand, the theory that physiochemical and especially endocrine processes are determining factors in what Schnitzler calls *Seelenzustände* has been accepted in general, although psychologists, psychiatrists, and investigators in physiological chemistry differ rather widely as to the particulars, such as the extent and the exact nature of these influences.

[15] Schnitzler himself belongs to this category. There is no doubt whatever as to his "poetic aptitude"—his entire work is evidence of that; and his great interest in, and knowledge of, psychology have been acknowledged repeatedly by experts, first among whom was Sigmund Freud himself. In a letter to Professor Josef Körner in Prague, dated July 27, 1927, Schnitzler mentions that he considered himself, in terms of mentality, "not a poet but a scientist (an author with a predominantly psychological orientation)." (In the posthumous papers, File No. 20.)

[16] Schnitzler used the French term *commis voyageur* because it has among German-speaking people a distinctly derogatory connotation. Literally, it means "traveling salesman."